THE LIFE OF SOTAESAN

THE FOUNDING MASTER OF WON BUDDHISM

THE LIFE OF
SOTAESAN

THE FOUNDING MASTER OF WON BUDDHISM

Venerable Wolsan

IlWon Publications

The Life of Sotaesan
The Founding Master of Won Buddhism

Published by IlWon Publications
361 Route 23, Claverack, NY 12513, USA
Phone: 518-851-2581

Library of Congress Control Number: 2024934137
ISBN: 979-8-9869466-6-5

Cover design by Kathy Abeyatunge
Printed in the Republic of Korea

CONTENTS

TRANSLATORS' FOREWORD

Helen Keller became both blind and deaf from scarlet fever when she was only nineteen months old. At the age of seven, Annie Sullivan, a teacher who was herself visually impaired, came and taught her sign language. It was a day Keller called: "the birthday of my soul."

At age fourteen, Keller was also fortunate to find spiritual guidance in the writings of the Swedish sage, Emanuel Sweden-borg, whom the great Japanese Zen Master D. T. Suzuki referred to as "The Buddha of the North."

Keller became the first deaf-blind person to earn a BA degree from an American university, graduating summa cum laude from Harvard's Radcliffe College. She became a renowned author, speaker, social activist, and philanthropist.

Helen Keller overcame her physical disabilities because she found great teachers who taught her how to live a life of service and inspiration in the world.

Those who are blind and deaf in their minds and hearts also need a spiritual guide who can enable them to see the path to eternal life: the way to ever-lasting and indestructible happiness and freedom. They also need a teacher who can plant the seed of grand vision in their minds and hearts and instill great aspiration for their present and future lives.

Keller spoke the truth of her own life experience when she said: "The only thing worse than being blind is having sight but no vision."

These days, orphanages in developed countries obtain plenty of funding from government assistance and corporate support. However, despite receiving adequate care, there still seems to be a sense of gloom on the faces of the children. They have plenty of food and clothing, yet the need for attention and warmth from loving caregivers is evident in their faces.

Venerable Daesan, the Third Head Dharma Master of

Won Buddhism, said, "The practitioners who do not have a teacher are like spiritual orphans." Some readers who have been attending temple services or practicing with a community for a long time, may still be spiritual orphans since they do not have a teacher or mentor.

Teachers are like gardeners. A tree, even a splendid tree, grows healthier when it receives proper care. Similarly, a practitioner's progress is far better when guided by a teacher. Awakened teachers are like those who stand at the top of the mountain peak. They have a broader perspective and deeper insight.

Imagine a magnificent mountain range with many foothills and peaks. Enlightened teachers are standing on higher crests than we are, and therefore, have a far more expansive vision. They can guide us to our destination through the most direct and efficient route. Sotaesan, the founding teacher of Won Buddhism, said, "I didn't even graduate from elementary school, and have little knowledge of the world, but I know how to make you a buddha."

This book is the translation of Venerable Wolsan's book, "Introduction to Won Buddhism" Chapter Two with Reverend Dosung Yoo's additional explanations.

It is our sincere wish that this book instills in readers a new perception of their life and a transformative vision for their future.

It is our prayer that all practitioners discover their own teacher, so they are guided to the path of perpetual and indestructible happiness and freedom.

Reverend Dosung Yoo and Kathy Abeyatunge
Won Dharma Center, 2024

CHAPTER 1

INTRODUCTION

Sotaesan, the Founding Master of Won Buddhism

SOTAESAN
THE FOUNDING MASTER OF
WON BUDDHISM

Sotaesan (1891-1943) is the founding master of Won Buddhism, who was enlightened to the Truth of Il-Won.

Sotaesan was born in 1891 to a peasant family in a small South Korean rural village. From the age of seven, he began to have persistent spiritual questions about nature and human life. He wondered, "How high is the sky?" "Where do the clouds and wind come from?" He questioned everything he observed, and each inquiry led to the next. The more engrossed he became in these countless spiritual questions, the more frustrated he grew because he lacked spiritual guidance.

At the age of eleven, Sotaesan attended a seasonal ceremony for the Remembrance of Ancestors, and there he heard a story about an omniscient mountain spirit. He hoped that meeting such a divine being would provide answers to all his spiritual questions. Every day for five years,

Sotaesan's birthplace in Youngsan

Sotaesan walked four kilometers from his home to the Sambat Mountain Pass and prayed to meet the mountain spirit, yet he never did, which intensified his frustration.

At the age of sixteen, Sotaesan heard an ancient tale about a person who had achieved enlightenment while practicing under a spiritual guide. For the next six years, he searched for a spiritual guide who could help him find the answers he was seeking. However, he was unable to find one.

By the time Sotaesan was twenty-two, he had stopped searching for a spiritual guide and instead had became deeply absorbed with one single thought: "What am I supposed to do?" During this time, he often entered deep

Sambat Pass where Sotaesan offered prayer in his early childhood

meditation, forgetting time and place and resting in the genuine realm of stillness.

On April 28th, 1916, after twenty years of searching for the truth, Sotaesan attained great enlightenment. He was twenty-six years old. That day marks the beginning of Won Buddhism.

After his enlightenment, Sotaesan read extensively

Sonjin Landing where Sotaesan entered deep meditaiton

from the scriptures of numerous religions. Upon reading the Diamond Sutra, he said, "Shakyamuni Buddha is truly the sage of sages. Although I have attained The Way without any teacher's guidance, looking back, from the time of my initial aspiration up to my final enlightenment, many aspects of my experience coincide with the practice and sayings of the Buddha in the past. For this reason, I regard Shakyamuni Buddha as my original teacher and the antecedent of my dharma. In the future, when I establish a religious order, I will create in this world a perfect and

Norumok where Sotaesan attained great enlightenment

complete dharma by taking the teachings of the Buddha as its core."

Sotaesan embraced the main tenets of the Buddha's teaching, but modernized and revitalized the traditional Buddhadharma to make it relevant and accessible to as many people as possible and to enrich their daily lives.

After his enlightenment, many people gathered to become his disciples and students. This newly created community organized a savings association under Sotaesan's direction.

In April 1918, using the funds, Sotaesan and his followers constructed a levee on a deserted, muddy beach in his hometown of Youngsan. The levee kept the salty sea water

Chongwanpyong, the farmland created by embankment project

at bay and its enclosed twenty-two acres eventually turned into fertile land. Crops were grown and sold to neighboring towns to provide a source of revenue and a means of subsistence for the developing Won Buddhist community.

In 1919, Sotaesan asked his nine disciples to offer a prayer for the deliverance of all beings. Through their selfless and sincere prayer, Won Buddhism received approval from the dharma realm.

From 1920 to 1924, at Bongnae-chongsa Hermitage, Sotaesan created a new dharma so that the followers of his teaching could attain and use the Great Way without leaving their secular lives.

In 1924, Sotaesan founded "The Society for the Study of Buddhadharma," a spiritual community with the mission of liberating all beings from suffering. This community flourished and later became the Headquar-

The former site of
Bongnae-chongsa Hermitage

Current Won Buddhism Headquarters

ters of Won Buddhism, where Sotaesan and his followers worked, practiced, and studied the dharma together under his new vision: "Daily life is Buddhadharma and Buddhadharma is daily life."

For twenty-eight years, Sotaesan worked tirelessly to spread the dharma and save all beings from suffering. On June 1, 1943, he passed away at the age of fifty-three.

Most scriptures from various spiritual traditions are transcriptions of oral transmissions. However, one of the distinguishing features of Won Buddhism is that Sotaesan wrote the Won Buddhist Scriptures himself. Until Sotaesan entered Nirvana, he meticulously edited and recorded his essential teachings, which are compiled in *The Principal Book of Won Buddhism*.

THE HISTORICAL BACKGROUND OF WON BUDDHISM

At the time of Sotaesan's birth in 1891, the world was experiencing a surge in colonization. As a result, smaller nations struggled to retain their independence while imperial powers sought to occupy them. Those occupying countries introduced what they termed as "civilized governance" and "modernity." The Korean people, in particular, endured a difficult era. Rife with internal corruption and disagreements among the ruling classes, the nation suffered from oppression, famine, and recurring diseases. This weakened state eventually led to Korea's colonization by Japan in 1910.

During this turbulent chapter in Korean history, many leaders pushed for social and political reform. However, Sotaesan perceived a more pressing matter: addressing the root causes of critical societal issues. He recognized that, alongside the inevitable march of scientific and technological progress, was an essential need to fortify the human mind. He was particularly concerned with the ailment of the human spirit, which was weakened by an overpowering inclination towards materialism. Sotaesan's insights were profound, highlighting the core reasons for civil, political, and social disturbances. He also offered a perspective on where the solution might lie.

The burden of finding a remedy for these issues weighed heavily on Sotaesan, causing him deep emotional unrest. Yet, this very state of agony paved the way for introspection and meditation, which ultimately lead him to a potential solution. Sotaesan encapsulated his belief in the phrase, "With this Great Unfolding of material civilization, Let there be a Great Unfolding of spirituality."

During this period, Sotaesan vowed to pursue enlightenment, attain Buddhahood and deliver all sentient beings from suffering. After attaining great enlightenment, he established a new religion, aiming for the grand salvation of humanity.

The rapid advancement of materialism and consumerism in contemporary society dominates people's minds, making them driven, competitive, and anxious. Sotaesan believed that the way to lead people to a happy life, free from suffering, is by empowering their minds and strengthening their spiritual capacities. This can only be done through faith in truthful dharma and realistic spiritual practice. That is why Won Buddhism emphasizes mind training practice.

In the movie 'Ben-Hur,' there is a dramatic naval battle scene where slaves are toiling beneath the ship's deck. During the battle, the ship experiences extensive damage and starts sinking. The slaves struggle to free themselves from their chains, but only the strong are able to break free and escape.

Just as physical strength allowed those strong slaves to break their physical chains, we need to cultivate our "mental strength" to shatter the various chains of ignorance that bind our minds and lives.

Breaking free and liberating ourselves from the invisible mental shackles of slavery in our lives is a task that all humans should embark upon.

Only through this inner transformation can we forge a path to an expansive and boundless paradise within our lives.

This is the founding motive of Won Buddhism.

WHAT IS WON BUDDHISM?

The name Won Buddhism (*Won-Bul-Kyo* in Korean) is a compound word for truth, enlightenment, and teaching. 'Won' means circle and symbolizes the ultimate truth. 'Bul' means enlightenment, and 'Kyo' means teaching the truth. Therefore, Won Buddhism is the path that leads us to become enlightened to the truth.

Sotaesan (1891-1943) attained great enlightenment in 1916 in Korea after many years of searching for the truth and engaging in many ascetic practices. He embraced the Buddha's teaching, yet he modernized and revitalized the traditional Buddhadharma so that many people in the secular world can utilize it to enrich their everyday lives.

After Sotaesan's great enlightenment, he created the image of Il-Won, also known as "One Circle," which symbolizes ultimate reality. Il-Won represents the origin of the universe and our original nature. All Won Buddhist temples enshrine this Il-Won image at the altar, as an object of faith and the model for practicing Won Buddhist teachings.

Sotaesan observed that humanity was becoming dominated by the rapid development and advancement of material civilization. Thus, he declared the founding motto of Won Buddhism: "With the great unfolding of material developments, let there be a great unfolding of spirituality."

The central teaching of Won Buddhism is the Fourfold Grace, Dharmakaya (Truth) Buddha, which consists of the Grace of Heaven and Earth, the Grace of Parents, the Grace of Fellow Beings, and the Grace of Laws.

The Fourfold Grace is fundamental to our efforts to transform this chaotic world into a peaceful one, as it expresses the interdependence of all beings.

In Won Buddhism, treating every living being as a buddha is an act of faith, as expressed in the motto: "Everywhere a Buddha, Every Act a Buddha Offering."

Won Buddhism teaches us how to use our mind.

Everything is of our mind's creation. This is the essence of the Buddha's teaching. Both the state of the world and the state of our lives are manifestations of our mind. Knowing how to use our mind is fundamental and is the key to a happy and fulfilling life. Therefore, mind practice, which teaches how to use the mind, is fundamental to Won Buddhist practice. Sotaesan said, "The study of any science has limits to its use, but if you learn how to make the mind function, this study can be utilized without a moment's interruption. Therefore, mind practice becomes the basis for all other studies." "If the mind is wholesome, everything wholesome arises along with it; if the mind is unwholesome, everything unwholesome arises along with it. Thus, the mind becomes the basis for everything wholesome and unwholesome."[1]

Timeless Meditation, Placeless Meditation is the essential path to mind practice, a way to practice meditation at all times, in every place. It teaches us how to maintain a peaceful, focused state of mind and how to use our original mind efficiently in our daily lives.

[1] *The Scriptures of Won-Buddhism*, 355.

Through Sotaesan's vision, traditional Buddhadharma was re-envisioned so that followers of Sotaesan could practice the path to enlightenment without abandoning their secular lives. Sotaesan said, "We do not want to be useless to the world because we are buddhist practitioners. Rather, we want to be very useful to our families, society, and our nation through the practical application of the Buddhadharma."

United Religions gather for World Peace.

Won Buddhism welcomes and embraces all people and all traditions of other faiths and strives to establish a World of Oneness in which all people live in harmony. With its open and inclusive teachings, Won Buddhism is working to realize the vision of United Religions as a counterpart of the United Nations.

CHAPTER 2

THE LIFE OF
MASTER SOTAESAN

SOTAESAN'S BIRTH AND EARLY CHILDHOOD

Sotaesan (1891-1943), the founding master of Won Buddhism, was enlightened to the Truth of Il-Won and established Won Buddhism in Korea.

Sotaesan's birthplace

Born in 1891 to a peasant family in a small South Korean village, he was a conscientious and magnanimous boy who carefully observed all natural phenomena. He also held great respect for his elders and took pleasure in asking them about their lives. Having an unwavering commitment to upholding the promises he made, Sotaesan was able to be steadfast and focused when faced with challenging situations.

Sotaesan's character is quite aptly illustrated in recounting two incidents from when he was just four years old.

In the late spring of 1896, in the small town of Young chon where Sotaesan was born, the whole village was in a state of anxiety over the impending approach of the Donghak Revolutionary Army which was under the command of General Chun Bong-Jun. The Donghak Army was composed of disgruntled peasants who held resentment towards the corrupt and exploitative practices of government authorities. Much of the population was afraid of the Donghak Revolutionary Army because thieves and rioters who often disguised themselves as Revolutionary soldiers. This band of soldiers killed and pillaged villages throughout the land. The adults in Sotaesan's life spoke about these events, and he listened very carefully.

One morning, Sotaesan was having breakfast with his father, Park Sung-sam, at their home in Norumok. Observing that his bowl had less rice compared to his father's, Sotaesan he took some rice from his father's bowl. His father light-heartedly admonished him, "You took from my bowl without asking, so you deserve to be punished." Sotaesan responded playfully by saying "If you decide to punish me, I'll surprise you first." Sotaesan's father was amused and did not pay much attention to Sotaesan's words.

After the meal, Park Sung-sam was resting in his room when all of a sudden Sotaesan shouted, "The Donghak Army is coming to Norumok! The Donghak Revolutionary Army is here!"

Park Sung-sam was so frightened by his son's shouting that he ran out of the room without even his shoes, and hid in the bamboo grove behind their house. After some time had passed, Sotaesan's mother decided to take a look around the village, but she found no sign of the

Donghak army anywhere. When she returned home, she asked Sotaesan whether or not the Donghak Army had actually come to Norumok. Sotaesan responded, "No, I just wanted to keep my word about surprising Father!" As such, since he was very young, he was determined to keep all the promises that he made, even if the circumstances were absurd.

Then, one summer day, when Sotaesan was five years old, he was playing in a creek near the village with his friends. His friends suddenly became very frightened, and some even burst out crying. Sotaesan stopped and asked his friends why they were so upset. With their hands trembling, the two other children pointed to a large snake lying in the grass nearby. Little Sotaesan approached the snake with a stick in his hand and shouted, "You mean snake! How dare you scare my friends!" In response to his loud shouting, the snake turned its head and slithered away into the bushes.

As such, little Sotaesan's boldness was often exhibited in his youth, and so people in his village called him the "small but bold child."

Seeking the Way

Questions Arise while Looking at the Sky.

At the early age of seven, Sotaesan grew deeply interested in the universal truths manifested in nature.

One day, he looked up at the clear sky and out at the surrounding mountains, which were filled with pure, clear energy. Suddenly, questions arose in his mind: "The sky is so high and vast, how did it become so clear?" and "How do the winds and clouds arise so unexpectedly from these clear skies?"

Filled with extraordinary curiosity, his mind continued to give rise to questions such as these. From the age of nine, he began to look inward and reflect deeply. Thus, his own existence became the subject of his contemplation.

Seeking the answers to all life's questions became the focus of his every waking hour. When he thought of his parents and his siblings, questions arose about them too. When he observed the change of day to night, that then became the object of his inquiry. His own incessant questioning left him often deeply restless and frustrated.

Oknyo-Bong mountain where young Sotaesan raised spiritual questions

Searching for a Mountain Spirit

Sotaesan's parents sent him to a private Confucian school, but he did not concentrate on his studies. He was disinterested in playing with the other children and was only focused on solving the questions that arose in his mind. When Sotaesan was eleven years old, his family took him to an ancestral ritual at a mountain village, Maup. Sotaesan noted that they first performed a ceremony for a mountain spirit before holding the ancestral ritual. He asked one of his relatives, "Why do we have the mountain spirit ceremony before the ancestral rituals?"

The family member explained to him that the mountain spirit governs the mountain due to their immense power and omniscience. Upon hearing this, Sotaesan's enthusiasm surged, and he inquired if he could encounter the mountain spirit to seek answers to his myriad of questions. The relative responded affirmatively but emphasized that he would have to commit wholeheartedly and single-mindedly to the quest.

So, seeking the mountain spirit, Sotaesan trekked up Sambat Pass to offer his prayers. This modest mountain, located close to his residence, was two and a half miles away. Every single morning, he undertook this journey without informing his parents. During this time period, numerous wild tigers roamed the mountains, deterring even the bravest of adults.

Nonetheless, little Sotaesan remained resolute. Every day, he ascended Sambat Pass to offer prayers at Court Rock in hopes of encountering the mountain spirit. He also presented fruit offerings and reverently bowed in all

Court Rock where Sotaesan offered prayer in hopes to meet a mountain spirit

four directions. Young Sotaesan often did not head home until after the sun had set. There were even instances when he'd drift off to sleep at the base of Court Rock, only to awaken at dawn.

For five years, he maintained this ritual, never skipping a day, no matter the challenges or adverse weather. One day, when his mother discovered his relentless excursions to the mountain, she was profoundly touched by his dedication and earnestness. So, she supported Sotaesan's quest to learn all the mysteries of the universe.

Even though Sotaesan prayed faithfully for five years at Sambat Pass, he was never able to the mountain spirit.

At the age of fifteen, Sotaesan's father, Park Sung-sam, set up a marriage for him with Yang Ha-un, hoping that this would deter Sotaesan from his quest for enlightenment. Sotaesan married Yang Ha-un. However, Sotaesan's spiritual journey remained undeterred.

The next year, as he reached the age of sixteen, Sotaesan attended a New Year's celebration with his in-laws. During the gathering, he overheard tales of how Taoist sages achieved spiritual enlightenment through encounters with esteemed masters. This discussion of *The Story of Paktaebo* and *The Story of Cho-ung* inspired Sotaesan to seek wisdom directly from a great master. Upon returning home, he set his mind on following a different path. Although he was still determined to obtain the answers he sought, he let go of his fruitless search for the mountain spirit. Instead, he turned his mind toward meeting a sage. He thought to himself, "I have not seen the mountain spirit in these five years, despite all my effort and devotion. Therefore, I cannot be certain if the mountain spirit even exists. However, if I make an effort to search for a sage, like the characters in the stories, I should be able to discover one."

After returning home from his in-laws, Sotaesan put all his effort into finding his spiritual master.

Searching for His Spiritual Master

From the tales Sotaesan gleaned from his in-laws', these spiritual masters were described as having immense supernatural abilities, akin to deities. It was also said that locating them was a challenge because they could easily blend in and may appear as a mere ordinary beggar. Consequently, Sotaesan began investigating every beggar he encountered on the streets, and tried to determine if any of them were, in fact, revered spiritual masters.

One day, Sotaesan passed a beggar sitting in front of the entrance to a bar, who was reading a Chinese poem. The man said in a loud voice, "Who will awaken first from this deep dream?!" Intrigued and suspecting that this man might be a master, Sotaesan extended an invitation for dinner at his home. However, after engaging in a lengthy conversation, Sotaesan discerned that the man was simply an ordinary individual.

However, Sotaesan continued to seek the truth. Seeing this, his father Park Sung-sam began to support him on his spiritual journey to find a great master.

One day, a self-proclaimed master appeared in the village. When Sotaesan invited him to his family's home, the man said he would answer all of Sotaesan's questions under two conditions. First, Sotaesan should regard him as a great master and treat him with appropriate respect and courtesy. Second, he would receive an ox as payment for answering Sotaesan's questions.

Sotaesan and his father felt that if this master were able to answer Sotaesan's questions, it would be worth the price of an ox.

When they agreed, the "master" began to pray for two days and nights. He said that he was calling his guardian angel who would come to answer Sotaesan's questions. Unfortunately, the prayer did not work, and so the embarrassed "master" requested several more offerings from Park Sung-sam so that he could call upon his guardian angel with even more devotion. Despite all his effort and prayer, the angel did not appear even after three days. So, the man fled in the middle of the night.

In the subsequent years, Sotaesan dedicated considerable time and resources in pursuit of a spiritual master, but to no avail. At the age of twenty, Sotaesan faced the abrupt loss of his caring and encouraging father. This tragedy deeply impacted him. As he persevered in his quest for enlightenment, he now bore the added burden of providing for his family. He felt compelled to settle the debts his father had acquired while he supported Sotaesan's spiritual journey. Taking the advice of his uncle's friend, Sotaesan opened a seasonal fish market on the Imjado and Tari Islands to make money. The markets proved to be a success. This endeavor helped Sotaesan pay back the debts. Still his spiritual questions loomed in his mind, and his desire to find the truth only grew deeper.

What am I supposed to do?

At the age of twenty-two, Sotaesan gave up searching for a spiritual guide who would answer the many questions which had plagued him from an early age. Instead, all his thoughts came together to formulate one single question, "What am I supposed to do?" He was deeply absorbed by this question day and night. Due to this ceaseless preoccupation, his daily life became more difficult, and he often looked like a man who was lost and without direction.

During this time, Sotaesan frequently entered into deep meditation. Time and place did not exist there and he began resting in the genuine realm of stillness. Sotaesan would stop while walking and sit like a stone. It was as if he was lost, unaware of himself or his surroundings.

These meditative states continued for a couple of years.

One early morning, Sotaesan waited for a ferry at Sonjin Landing to go to the market across the river. While waiting, he entered into great Samadhi and stood in absolute calmness until the sun had set.

As people made their way home from the market at dusk, they stumbled upon

Sonjin Landing where Sotaesan entered deep Samadhi

Sotaesan, standing motionless. They exclaimed, "Hey, Sotaesan! Why are you still here?" Startled by their calls, Sotaesan woke up.

Sotaesan frequently found himself profoundly engrossed in pondering, "What is my purpose?" His concentration was such that he'd stand motionless on the road for extended periods of time. He remained oblivious to his surroundings. He would often suffer sunburns from being exposed to the intense summer sun for hours on end.

One day, his wife prepared breakfast for him in the early morning before she went out to the field to work. When she returned home around lunch time, she discovered Sotaesan still sitting silently at the breakfast table, absorbed in deep meditation. Even though countless flies buzzed around his bowl of rice, he remained undisturbed.

From the age of twenty-five, the single thought "What am I supposed to do?" began to disappear, and he entered into a deeper samadhi. During this time, he began to develop an intermittent cough, and an abscess formed on his skin. His body also broke out into a rash due to the excessive sun exposure he received.

When neighbors saw Sotaesan in such a state, they were reluctant to approach him as they thought he might have a contagious disease. By most, he was considered insane due to the state of his appearance and his samadhi experiences. Thus, people not only avoided his presence, but also his home. Furthermore, Sotaesan's house was also in great need of repair, causing his family circumstances to become more difficult.

THE GREAT ENLIGHTENMENT

In the early morning hours of April 28, 1916, Sotaesan sat in deep meditation. As he meditated in his house in Norumok village, his mind and heart suddenly became refreshed and open. By daybreak, his mind had completely cleared.

He immediately left his room and looked out into the clear starlit sky of dawn, and felt a sensation unlike any he had experienced before. Strolling through the courtyard near his house, he reflected on the hardship of previous years. Sotaesan, then, felt the need to comb his hair and cut his nails. He carefully washed his face and when the sun began to shine brightly, he searched for something he could use to clean his body. Once finished, he saw the state of his home and felt the same need to clean what was disheveled and fix everything in need of repair.

At this time, the boils on his body began to disappear as

well, revealing clear and smooth skin. After eating breakfast, Sotaesan overheard a discussion between a few neighbors regarding the contents of the *Tong-kyong Taejon* (Great Canon of Eastern Learning), which states: "I, the Heavenly Lord, have a sacred amulet. Its name is Miraculous Medicine, and its form is the Great Circle." Immediately, upon hearing this passage, Sotaesan clearly understood its meaning.

Later, two Confucian scholars passed by Sotaesan's house. They took rest there and discussed a passage in the *I-Ching*, the Chinese philosophy book: "A great person is united with the virtue of Heaven and Earth, the brightness of the sun and the moon, the sequence of the four seasons, and unified with the good and ill-fortune of the spirit." When Sotaesan heard this passage, he also understood its meaning with perfect clarity.

Sotaesan recalled all the doubts and questions he had previously raised and realized their meaning with the same perfect clarity. He felt inexpressible joy. He had finally achieved great enlightenment.

After his great enlightenment, Sotaesan expressed his state of mind in a verse: "When the moon rises as a fresh breeze blows, the myriad of forms become naturally clear."

Norumok in Youngsan where Sotaesan attained great enlightenment

Sotaesan also declared, "All beings are of a single nature and all things originate from one source. The Truth of neither arising nor ceasing and the karmic principle of cause and effect operate in perfect harmony, in an interrelated system."

This was his first dharma instruction—the truth to

which he had awakened.

This means that the principle of the universe is fundamentally one: the permanent aspect of universal truth or eternal life, is inseparable from the impermanent aspect of universal truth, which is the karmic principle of cause and effect. Together, these elements form a unified reality.

Sotaesan realized that our primal awareness, our universal consciousness, is everlasting, and all things are continuously changing. Whatever goes, comes again. Whatever comes, goes again. Those who give will receive, and those who receive will eventually give.

However, this awakening was not limited to Sotaesan's own personal

Young Sotaesan

experience. His awakened mind and heart became filled with great empathy and compassion. Sotaesan, as a result, sought to reach out with helping hands in order to deliver all sentient beings from suffering.

SPREADING THE DHARMA

Gathering Disciples

Following his enlightenment, Sotaesan underwent a profound transformation. He exuded virtue and compassion like never before. His demeanor carried immense grace, and a luminous radiance surrounded him. This striking change drew individuals towards him, and within a few months, he had amassed a following of forty people.

In 1917, one year after Sotaesan attained great enlightenment, he devised a method to organize his followers in a manner to teach people effectively. This method is referred to as the Kyohwa-dahn, which is the dharma study/practice group that consists of nine members and one leader.

Sotaesan became the leader of the first Kyohwa-dahn. He selected eight disciples who had sincere and strong faith. The first disciples were: Lee Jae-chol, Lee Sun-sun,

Kim Ki-chon, Oh Chang-gon, Park Se-chol, Park Dong-guk, Yu Keon, Kim Kwang-son.

However, Sotaesan left the position for the central member vacant. He said "There is a certain person meant for this position. That person will come soon and help us greatly."

The first nine disciples of Sotaesan

After the Kyohwa-dahn was created, Sotaesan made a mindfulness journal book named, *Sungye-myongshi-rok* and suggested that the disciples spend ten days writing down what and how they have studied and practiced. Thus, they examined the strengthening or weakening of their faith, as well as how they put their faith into action. Initially, this practice evoked a blend of apprehension and intrigue among them. However, they soon recognized that the act of journaling helped immensely to fortify their faith and commitment. The disciples held steadfast belief

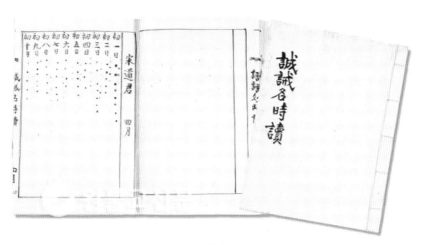

Sungye-myongshi-rok, the first mindfulness journal book

in Sotaesan's teachings and followed him with profound dedication.

One day, Sotaesan encouraged his disciples to create a savings association, stating, "For us to study and engage in spiritual practice, we must unite and generate income." So, this newly created community followed his direction and organized the savings association. To establish a new religious order, the savings association provided a base of financial support to prepare for future dharma work.

Establishing a Savings Association

In order to save money for this great undertaking, each of Sotaesan's followers made an effort to abstain from drinking alcohol and smoking tobacco. They also worked on holidays and saved the extra income. Additionally, they saved some money by ending expensive memorial rituals which were traditionally offered to the realm of truth. The disciples' wives also helped by saving a small portion of rice, called 'gratitude rice'. All these efforts paved the way for establishing a financially secure community for spiritual practice.

This also served as a way to open and empower their minds and hearts for spiritual awakening and to change the difficult circumstance of their lives under Japanese rule.

Subsequently, Sotaesan recommended using their accumulated savings, along with borrowed funds from an affluent neighbor and money he obtained from selling his household furniture, to buy charcoal. A few months later, during World War I, the demand for charcoal surged, causing its price to skyrocket. Consequently, within a year, the community savings association garnered significant wealth, yielding a profit that was a tenfold increase from their initial expectations.

Having a great sense of responsibility for the money, Sotaesan said, "With the money we have earned together, we can now carry out an important project which I've had in mind. Please listen and contemplate this."

Pointing to the riverside, Sotaesan said "Look at that tidal land! That piece of land has been deserted for a long time, but we could build a dam and transform that tidal land into a rice field. It will take several years to complete, but it will surely strengthen our community as well as our country. Let us start this project for the benefit of the public's welfare."

Embankment Project

The proposal from Sotaesan to construct an embankment at Youngsan surprised them. No one in thousands of years had ever conceived of such an endeavor.

The disciples showed an unwavering faith in Sotaesan and decided to unite and carry out the reclamation project.

This event marked a pivotal chapter both in Won Buddhism and the annals of religious history. No religious faction had ever undertaken such an initiative before. This took place three years after Sotaesan's enlightenment.

When the embankment project began, Sotaesan went out to sea and measured the depth required to drive the posts securely in place. Then the disciples connected the posts with straw ropes to establish the area of the dam. Next, Sotaesan asked his followers to cut pine trees and bring them over to the seashore to build the levee.

This project began only a few months after the savings association had started, yet, the embankment project was remarkably efficient.

Still, the project's execution was fraught with challenges. The magnitude of the task was unprecedented for the villagers. Many mocked the laborers and voiced their profound doubts.

One day, a member of a nearby religious group, who was the brother of Sotaesan's friend, mocked them, saying, "When our teaching has been widely spread, it would be easy to give you the position of local governor. So, it would

Embankment project, 1919

be better to stop this construction and simply donate the money to our local church instead."

Yet, some of the local people were very supportive and offered words of encouragement. One such person stood up to the naysayers and said, "My dear fellows, don't speak that way. After seeing Sotaesan create the savings union and run the charcoal business, I am certain that it is quite possible for this project to become a success."

As the construction advanced, financial constraints became a hurdle. Faced with this challenge, Sotaesan found himself seeking external sources from which to borrow the necessary funds.

One day, Sotaesan told his disciple, Kim Ki-chon to pay a visit to Kim Deok-il, a rich man in the village, to borrow money. Kim Deok-il was a well-known loan shark and a miser, who never loaned money without a guarantee and good return on his investment. Kim Ki-chon said to Sotaesan, "He will never loan us the money without security. It's just not possible." Sotaesan said, "Go meet with him. He will be happy to give us the loan."

Kim Ki-chon followed Sotaesan's instruction, and visited Kim Deok-Il even though he had some doubts and uncertainty. When Kim Ki-chon asked for the loan, much to his surprise, Kim Deok-il was happy to offer the money. It was as if he had been waiting for him. The very next day he came to the embankment site with the money he had promised.

On April 26, 1919, a year after its commencement, the embankment project came to fruition. Despite facing numerous challenges and enduring persistent critique, the order successfully transformed around 25 acres of tidal territory into arable farmland. Sotaesan named this farmland *Chongwanpyong*, which translates as "the land for reflecting on purity and righteousness."

The tidal lands in Youngsan, where the embankment project was carried out

This farmland became the economic foundation of the initial stage of Won Buddhism. While the embankment project was at the peak of its construction, Song Kyu, who later became the second Head Dharma Master of Won Buddhism, arrived to join the order.

For an extended period, Sotaesan had keenly anticipated Song Kyu's arrival. Upon his entry, Song Kyu assumed a pivotal role within the Kyohwa-dahn, the dharma study and practice group. Later, they built the first temple at the foot of Ongnyo Peak and named it *Gugwan-dosil*, meaning "nine-room house."

Young Chongsan who later became the Second Head Dharma Master

Relying on the Will of Universal Truth

In March 1919, precisely when the embankment project was nearing completion, Korea witnessed a non-violent uprising against Japanese colonization. Known as the March 1st Independence Movement, this protest rapidly gained traction across the nation. Many of Sotaesan's disciples felt compelled to participate in the demonstrations.

When some of his disciples asked Sotaesan, "What should we do at this time?" Sotaesan replied, "This is the sound that resonates, the call for the Great Unfolding of the future. It is the voice of people wishing for a new world. Let us hurry to finish the embankment project and pray for this world."

During this time, Sotaesan had a grander vision in mind. It was to deliver all sentient beings through the Buddhadharma. However, in order to accomplish this, he needed to first obtain dharma authentication from the realm of truth.

Sotaesan told his disciples, "It is our responsibility to prepare ourselves so that we can help deliver all people from suffering. His disciples followed his direction and set out to pray with utmost sincerity and devotion. They first prepared themselves by washing and purifying their body and mind. Then they climbed to the peaks of the Kusu Mountains which Sotaesan had designated for them.

On April 28, the three-year anniversary of Sotaesan' great enlightenment, they began praying. This was also the same day the embankment project was completed. Thereafter, they prayed three times a month, and for the nine following days they did their best to live with a pure mind and heart in accordance with the prayer they offered.

The former site of the Nine-Room House

On prayer days, they all gathered in the dharma room of the nine-room house where they received instructions from Sotaesan. They then departed for their designated prayer sites. Each member was given a watch so that they could synchronize their prayer time, and each was assigned a mountaintop as the site of their prayer. At the peak of the mountains, each member carefully arranged his prayer site by setting up a flag at their respective location, preparing incense and a bowl of clear water, bowing, reading the prayer, and reciting a chanting phrase.

The prayer offered was as follows:

I, offer this prayer wholeheartedly to the Fourfold Grace: the Grace of Heaven and Earth, the Grace of Parents, the Grace of Fellow Beings, and the Grace of Laws.

Human beings are the masters of all things; all things should be utilized by human beings. The Way of humanity is grounded on benevolence and righteousness, while deceptive tactics are erroneous. Therefore, it is appropriate that the human spirit naturally utilize all material things and establish the great Way of benevolence and righteousness throughout the world. Currently, however, benevolence and righteousness have lost their influence, and deceptiveness has claimed dominion over the world. As a consequence, establishing the great Way has become fraught with obstacles. Now is the time when we must join our minds and hearts together and act in concert to rectify both the ways of the world and the human mind, which are declining day by day. We hope and pray that we will uphold the sacred intention and aspiration of Sotaesan and solidify the dharma connection between ourselves and our community. We vow that the right dharma will be established to rectify the declining human spirit.

We sincerely ask the Fourfold Grace to respond to our prayers and to help us accomplish our goal with its boundless power and infinite grace.

This prayer was offered from 10:00 pm until 12:00 am. Afterwards, everyone returned to the nine-room house.

After three months of prayer, Sotaesan said to his disciples, "The devotion and sincerity with which you have prayed is truly praiseworthy. However, I can see that it is not sufficient to move the realm of truth. This is because there still remains some defilement of ego left in your minds. If extinguishing your ego can help establish the correct dharma, will you carry out that task?" To this, the nine disciples said in unison, "Yes, we will."

Sotaesan continued more solemnly, "There's an age-old adage that says, 'To uphold one's virtue and to manifest benevolence, one must sometimes sacrifice oneself for a noble cause.' There have been those who achieved wonders by embracing this tenet. When one dedicates their life to the betterment of all living beings, how could the divine spirits of Heaven and Earth remain unmoved? Soon, a great Way grounded in the true dharma will flourish across the globe, rectifying the misguided perceptions of humanity. This shift will contribute a multitude of blessings to all sentient beings. Then, you will naturally become the saviors of the world, and your merit will become eternal. Therefore, truthfully express your views on this matter from your heart."

The nine disciples were downcast for a while, but in the end, they agreed wholeheartedly that they were willing to sacrifice their lives. With great admiration, Sotaesan highly praised them, and asked them to carry out the sacrifice at their designated prayer sites. This was to take place on the next prayer day, following the ten days of ablutions.[2]

On August 21, the nine disciples gathered in the dharma room, and at 8:00 pm Sotaesan asked them to arrange a bowl of clear water and place their daggers on the table. Also, on the table was a white sheet of paper on which was written their names and the words, "Sacrifice with no Regret." Sotaesan then asked each of them to press their bare thumb underneath their name to symbolize their signature. They were then asked to prostrate and offer a silent prayer affirming their determination to sacrifice their lives on behalf of all sentient beings. When finished, the disciples pressed their bare thumbs on the white paper.

Soon after, Sotaesan examined the paper, and saw that the places where the disciples had pressed their bare thumbs had turned into blood-stained fingerprints. Showing the paper to his disciples, he said, "Look at this paper.

2 *The Scripture of Wonbulkyo*, 1054-1055.

This is evidence of your single devoted heart and mind." He then burned the paper to consecrate it to the realm of truth and ordered his disciples to go to their prayer sites.

However, once they stepped out of the dharma room, Sotaesan called them back saying that he had one more thing to tell them. "The spirits of heaven and earth have already responded to your vow. The planning in the realm of dharma has now been completed. The success of our plan has been assured by your action. Your sacrifice has been acknowledged by the world." Hearing Sotaesan's words, the joy and excitement of the disciples could not be quelled for some time.

At 11:00 that night, Sotaesan asked the nine disciples to go to the top of Jung-ahng mountain to offer prayers. When they returned, Sotaesan assigned each of them a dharma name and a dharma title, saying, "The individual who held a secular name has died. Now I give you a new name. With this universal dharma name, you are reborn. I have called you back to life by bestowing on you this name for use throughout the world. Receive and cherish your dharma name with honor and try to deliver numerous sentient beings."

Jung-ahng mountain where Chongsan prayed

Hence, Sotaesan revitalized the spirits of the nine disciples. Through their willingness to sacrifice for the greater good, he ingrained a deep truth in them: *The purpose of our lives is to serve the well-being of all.*

The transformation of the nine disciples' fingerprints into blood seals is termed "the Event of Dharma Authentication." It was this significant act that granted Won Buddhism its dharma validation from the domain of universal truth. Today, the Day of Dharma Authentication stands as one of the four major annual observances in Won Buddhism.

Since the original nine disciples received their dharma names and dharma titles on this day, receiving a dharma name or dharma title has become a symbol of rebirth from a single secular being into a public figure. Adopting a dharma name signifies a commitment to the path of dharma. This act symbolizes an individual's renewed dedication to pursuing great enlightenment, aiming for the betterment of all living beings.

Creating Dharma for Future Generations

After the event of dharma authentication, Sotaesan asked his disciple, Song Kyu, to go to Zen Master Hakmyong (1867~1929) who resided at Wolmyong Hermitage. Master Hakmyong was a well-known and prominent Zen Master. Sotaesan wanted Song Kyu to become Hakmyong's attendant.

As Song Kyu was leaving, Sotaesan said, "Don't read Buddhist scriptures." Reflecting on this later, Song Kyu mentioned, "I adhered to Sotaesan's guidance and even made an effort to steer clear of the table where the scriptures were kept."

After sending off Song Kyu, Sotaesan began residing in Silsangsa Temple, which was one mile from Wolmyong Hermitage. As more disciples came to see him, they decided to build a thatched cottage for Kim Nam-chon and Song Jeok-byok. That residence was officially known as Bongaejeonsa, but was commonly called "Sukdu-am" Hermitage.

When Sotaesan first began his stay at Sukdu-am Hermitage, he told Song Kyu to terminate his service as the attendant to Master Hakmyeong and return to him.

Together with his disciples, Sotaesan began to formulate the core tenets of Won Buddhism, aiming to relieve all sentient beings from their anguish. For about five years prior to the establishment of the Won Buddhism Headquarters, he resided at Bongnae-chongsa Hermitage, where he continued to develop and refine his teachings to aid in the liberation of all beings from their suffering.

The outline of Sotaesan's new teaching was two-pronged: "The Essential Way of Human Life," encompassing "the Fourfold Grace" and "the Four Essentials," and "the Essential

Bongnae-chongsa Hermitage where Sotaesan composed the Won Buddhism Canon

Way of Practice," incorporating "the Threefold Practice" and "the Eight Articles." These teachings offered a refreshed and modernized interpretation of traditional Buddhadharma, which allowed adherents to grasp and embody the Great Way without abandoning their everyday lives.

Construction of Headquarters

Sotaesan traveled to Byeonsan, driven by two main objectives. First, he aimed to craft a modern dharma suited for contemporary society. Secondly, he sought to build strong connections and relationships with a vast number of individuals.

While Sotaesan spent five years at Bongnae-chongsa Hermitage, numerous individuals from various regions sought him out in their quest for enlightenment. Later, when it came time for Sotaesan to found the Headquarter, several of these visitors became instrumental in shaping the foundational practice community. Among them was a follower named Seo Jung-an. Although he was ten years older than Sotaesan, Seo Jung-an sincerely asked, "Please

Sotaesan and his students in the early days of Won Buddhism, 1928

allow me to call you father." Such a request was unusual, so Sotaesan felt uncomfortable and refused. But, with heartfelt insistence, Seo Jung-an pleaded with Sotaesan to change his mind.

One day, when Seo Jung-an visited Sotaesan at Bongnae Mountain, he made a very important observation, saying, "The road in this area is too rocky and this hermitage is too small. In my humble opinion, you should move to an area that is more easily accessible and has adequate space. This would make it far easier to help guide people in the future." Sotaesan then sensed that the time had come for him to create a new spiritual community, which would be the first step in opening a new religious practice. Thus, he agreed with Seo Jung-an and consented to move his residence.

On June 1, 1914, a meeting was held at Bokwang Buddhist Temple in Iksan to form The Society for the Study of Buddhadharma (later renamed Won Buddhism). From that day, The Society for the Study of Buddhadharma was established in the Shin-rong district in Iksan as a spiritual community where all Sotaesan's followers worked, studied and practiced dharma together. The city of Iksan's convenient location along a central traffic route made the community more accessible.

In November, they constructed two wooden huts with thatched roofs, which marked the beginning of the

Won Buddhism Headquarters

new spiritual community. However, after erecting these structures, the community faced significant financial challenges. To generate funds, they started a taffy business. They also adopted frugal measures, often subsisting on acacia leaves or taffy rice. Moreover, they took on roles as tenant farmers, leasing modest pieces of land to grow crops and fruit trees.

One day, the renowned freedom fighter Ahn Chang-ho, who had recently been released from prison for his role in the Korean independence movement, visited The Society for the Study of Buddhadharma. Sotaesan warmly welcomed him, commending him for the sacrifices he had made for the Korean people.

Ahn Chang-ho, freedom fighter for Korean liberation, 1936

Ahn Chang-ho said, "What I am doing is small in scope and short in skill, bringing little benefit to the nation and even leading to the persecution of many of my comrades by the colonial police. But what you, sir, are doing is vast in scope and proficient in its expedience, as you contribute greatly to this cause without anyone being persecuted or put under restraint. How I truly admire your ability!"

Given that Ahn Chang-ho was under surveillance by the Japanese police, he kept his conversation with Sotaesan short. Still, however, after his visit, the local police intensified their monitoring of The Society for the Study of Buddhadharma. The Japanese officials sought to dismantle the newly formed spiritual community. As part of their strategy, they set up a police substation within the Headquarters

Sotaesan and Japanese policemen

and secretly placed an undercover officer within the Won community. They meticulously monitored The Society's activities around the clock, sending police and detectives to Headquarters in search of any illicit activities. However, their internal investigation did not find any proof of illegal acts being committed.

Sotaesan was also summoned several times to the police station for interrogation. Despite all the hardships, he continued to pour a great deal of effort into training his followers to become seasoned practitioners and great dharma teachers.

By 1924, Sotaesan had established the spiritual community at Shinyong, Iksan; there he worked ceaselessly until his death. He worked with great dedication and sincerity to help alleviate suffering for all people. Sotaesan emphasized that a living religion or practice should not be separate from our daily lives. The essence of his

Gongwhedang where Sotaesan delivered his dharma discourses

teaching was "Buddhadharma is Daily Life, Daily Life is Buddhadharma."

In 1925, Sotaesan conducted the first meditation retreat based on the newly established method of dharma practice. Due to the limited size of the houses available at the Headquarters at that time, he temporarily rented a space in Jeon Eumkwang's home. This space was used to conduct summer meditation sessions. Approximately ten male and female members participated in these retreats, and were guided by Song Kyu. Song Kyu later would become Sotaesan's dharma successor.

Winter retreat with Sotaesan, 1930

In November, a winter meditation retreat was held for approximately twenty male and female members. This retreat was directed and guided by Lee Chun-pung. These two meditation retreats were the beginning of what would eventually be regarded as the regular dharma retreats for Won Buddhism.

Through such trainings or retreats, Sotaesan refined his

Sotaesan and his students, 1941

new dharma to open the minds and hearts of all suffering people and to deliver all sentient beings.

Such regular retreats not only served as important periods for lay members to train themselves in the study and practice of the dharma, but also served as the only means to train the ministers in the early days of Won Buddhism. A community hall was later constructed and used as the place of training.

Nirvana

Preparation for His Passing

For several years before his death, Sotaesan would often say to his students, "I will leave soon for self-cultivation. Reflect on whether or not you will regress in my absence. Fortify your minds."

When he spoke, his students did not think that he was referring to his impending death. Instead, some thought to themselves, "Sotaesan is a true and great sage, free from birth and death. We will follow him, wherever he goes."

In the Great Enlightenment Hall on January 28, 1941, two years before his death, Sotaesan gave the congregation his transmission verse which summarized his enlightenment experience.

The transmission verse is as follows:

"Being into nonbeing, and nonbeing into being,

Great Enlightenment Hall, Won Buddhism Headquarters

Turning and turning in the ultimate,

Being and nonbeing are both empty,

Yet this emptiness is also complete."

When Sotaesan delivered his transmission verse, he
said, "Although enlightened masters of the past disclosed

their transmission verse on their deathbeds to only a few of their students, I am handing down this transmission verse now in advance for all people. Whether you receive the dharma or not depends entirely on your study and practice. Therefore, each of you should carry out your study and practice so that you will have no regret later."

He also explained his transmission verse with the following words, "Being is a realm of change; nonbeing is a realm of unchanging. Yet, this is a realm that cannot be called either being nor nonbeing. It is also expressed as 'turning and turning' and 'ultimate', but these are only expressions provided as a way of teaching. So, what is the point of saying 'both empty' or 'complete'? Since this realm is the true essence of our original nature, do not try to understand it through rationalizations; rather, you should awaken to this realm through contemplation."

To prepare the dharma for after his death, Sotaesan also delivered the newly designed Won Buddhist doctrinal chart and said:

"The quintessence of my teachings and dharma lies herein; however, how many of you can understand my true inten-

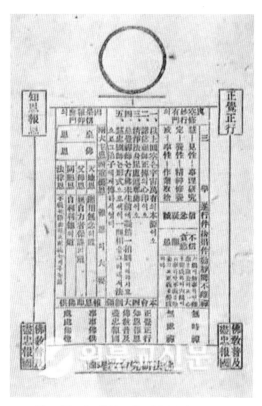

The Chart of Won Buddhist doctrine

tion? It seems that only a few of you in this congregation today can receive it fully. This is first due to your minds being attached to wealth and sex, and secondly, your inclination toward reputation and vanity, which has prevented you from one-minded concentration. With this, you must decide what to leave behind and what to seek. You will find success only by making a big decision and taking just a single path."[3]

He also emphasized three goals of the organization: spreading the dharma, education, and charity. He said, "In the future, we must always promote these three in tandem so that our initiative may be flawless."

A year before his nirvana, Sotaesan often urged his disciples to complete the compilation of *The Principal Book of Won Buddhism*, which was in progress. He would often stay up late at night editing the work.

When the manuscript was completed, he had it sent immediately to the printers, saying to his disciples:

"Since time is short, the book may not be complete, but the essence of my whole life's aspiration and vision are basically expressed in this one volume. Therefore, please receive and keep this book so that you may learn through its words, realize with your own mind, and practice with your body. Let this dharma be transmitted forever, throughout

3   Ibid, 402-403.

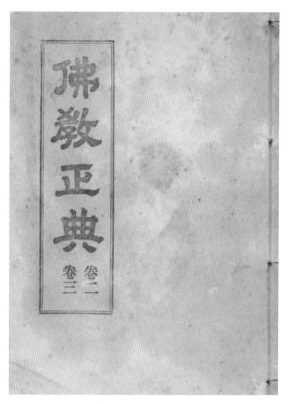

The original Won Buddhism Canon, 1943

tens of thousands of generations. In the future, people throughout the world, will recognize this dharma and be deeply impressed. Countless people will hold this dharma in reverence."[4]

4 Ibid, 400.

Sotaesan also said:

"It is vital that you transmit my dharma to future generations by writing it down and explaining it orally. However, it is more important for you to put the dharma into practice and realize it with your minds, so this dharma lineage is never severed. If you do so, your merit will be beyond measure."[5]

His Passing

On May 16, 1943, Sotaesan presented his final dharma talk.

"On my way here to the Dharma Hall, I met several children who were playing in the woods by the side of the road. Upon seeing me, one of them signaled to the others, and together they all stood up and bowed. From their behavior, it was apparent they were maturing. When people

5   Ibid, 407-408.

are very young, they don't understand the nature of family relationships or their responsibilities to family members. As they mature, this becomes more apparent. Likewise, when practitioners are ignorant, they do not understand the particulars of how one becomes a buddha, bodhisattva, or ordinary sentient being, or the understanding of relationships between themselves and heaven and earth, the myriad of living things, or the pathway between birth and death. As their practice gradually evolves, they come to understand the Truth. Therefore, in the same manner that a child gradually becomes an adult, we come to understand the Way; an ordinary human being awakens and becomes a buddha and a disciple learns and becomes a master. This means that you must acquire more knowledge through learning so that you can teach the younger generations, thus become pioneers in delivering all sentient beings and curing the world of suffering. It is said in the *Yin-fu ching* (Dark Amulet Scripture), 'Birth is the root of death; death is the root of birth.' Birth and death are like the rotation of the four seasons and the recurrence of day and night. All things in the universe operate on the principle of Truth. Buddhas and bodhisattvas are not ignorant about birth and death; rather they are free from them, unlike ordinary sentient beings who are constrained by them. However, the births and deaths of the physical bodies of buddhas and bodhisattvas or ordinary sentient beings are all the same. Therefore, believe in both the persona and dharma, and work hard to gain freedom from delusion regarding birth and death, coming and going. We hold regular dharma meetings so that the participants can be of service to each other, sharing knowledge and experience to gain insight and grow. Be careful not to come and go in vain; the matter of birth and death is great and change occurs rapidly. It is not something to be taken lightly."[6]

That Sunday morning, Sotaesan seemed well and hearty. After the dharma service, he partook in his usual lunch of steamed rice wrapped in leafy greens. However, as the afternoon progressed, he experienced chest discomfort, and his countenance turned pale and feeble. After the doctor's examination, Sotaesan was diagnosed with cerebral anemia. The doctor administered an injection of cam-

6   Ibid, 405-407.

phor to produce a stimulating effect in the chest to increase the red blood cell count. Nevertheless, his condition continued to deteriorate. His disciples implored him to go to the hospital, but he refused and insisted that he would be fine. Ten days later, on May 27th, he was taken to Iri Hospital and treated by Dr. Wakaski. The treatment was of no avail, and Sotaesan entered into nirvana. He was fifty-three years old. It was June 1, 1943, two years before Korea's liberation from Japanese rule.

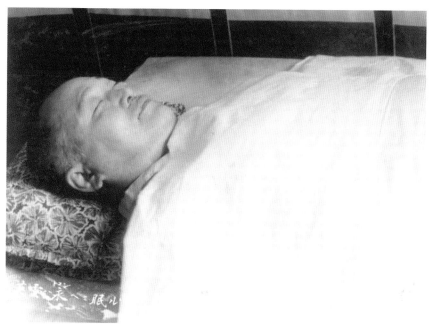

Sotaesan passes into Nirvana, 1943

Sotaesan led and taught his students selflessly for twenty-eight years after he had attained great enlightenment. When he entered nirvana, the Japanese police were relieved and said, "Sotaesan, the Gandhi of Korea has left. Now The Society of the Study of Buddhadharma will perish."

Before and after the funeral service, his disciples witnessed several miracles. His body emitted light and the smell of incense lingered. Ten days after his cremation, the Headquarters emitted a glow as if it were on fire. The light was so bright that some disciples rushed from Iri Station, which was two miles away, to put the fire out.

Sotaesan's funeral service, the Great Englightenemnt Hall, 1943

His disciples scheduled the public memorial to be held for nine days. The Japanese police did not permit the ceremonies to continue as planned, and the mourning period was reduced to six days. The funeral service itself was held on June 6, 1943, six days after his passing, in the Great Enlightenment Hall. The number of attendants for the funeral procession was limited to two-hundred. Fifty-five people shouldered the bier carrying his casket to the crematorium.

Soteasan's funeral procession

During that era, it was a prevalent tradition that when a Buddhist master passed into nirvana, his disciples would seek out sari from the ashes after cremation. These crystals are regarded as sacred relics, symbolizing the achievement of profound enlightenment. While Sotaesan was alive, he would often say, "I will not leave behind any Sari. Do not try to search for anything mysterious or mystical from me. If there are such disciples who engage in this, they are not my true disciples."

As promised, Sotaesan's passing followed the natural course of human existence. This embodies the core principles of practice and human life: the Way is found in the ordinary. Such was the manner in which he both lived and departed.

The Japanese authorities closely monitored the cremation ceremony until its conclusion. They prohibited the disciples from bringing his ashes into the Headquarters. Following the 49th day of the service commemorating Sotaesan's deliverance, his ashes were placed in a public graveyard. The inscription on his tombstone bore the words, "Il-Won Master Sotaesan."

The pagoda where Sotaesan's ashes are enshrined

When Korea was liberated from Japan in 1945, his ashes were moved to the Won Buddhism Headquarters. On April 25, 1949, the sacred pagoda of Sotaesan was erected to memorialize his life.

Chongsan, the Second Head Dharma Master

1. QUESTIONING EVERYTHING

In 1891, Sotaesan, the Founding Master of Won Buddhism, was born to a simple peasant family who lived in a small rural village in Southern Korea. From the age of seven, many questions about nature and human life arose in his mind. He wondered, "Why do clouds and wind form in a calm and clear sky?" and "Why do mothers and fathers have such a close relationship?" He questioned everything he observed; one question led to another. Those countless questions filled Sotaesan's mind and launched his spiritual journey.

2. OFFERING PRAYER AT SAMBAT PASS

At the age of eleven, Sotaesan attended a seasonal ceremony for the Remembrance of Ancestors, where he heard a story about an omniscient mountain spirit. He hoped that meeting such a divine being would answer all of his spiritual questions.

Every day for five years thereafter, he traveled four kilometers from his house to climb Sambat Pass and pray fervently to meet a mountain spirit. His sincerity and dedication greatly empowered his mind and laid the spiritual foundation that would later enable him to enter deep meditation.

3. SEARCHING FOR A SPIRITUAL GUIDE

At the age of sixteen, Sotaesan heard an ancient story about a person who had achieved enlightenment by practicing under a spiritual guide.

By this time, he had given up his search for a mountain spirit. For the next six years, he searched for a spiritual guide who could answer the questions he contemplated. Although he was not able to find a guide, his earnest will and devotion eventually led him to become a spiritual teacher himself.

4. ENTERING DEEP MEDITATION

At the age of twenty-two, Sotaesan gave up searching for a spiritual guide who could answer the many questions that had plagued his mind from a young age.

Consequently, he became deeply absorbed in one single thought: "What am I supposed to do?" During this time, he often entered into deep meditation, forgetting time and place, and resting in the realm of genuine stillness.

One early morning while waiting for a ferry at Sonjin Landing, he entered into great Samadhi and stood in absolute calmness throughout the entire day.

5. GREAT ENLIGHTENMENT AT NORUMOK

In the early morning of April 28, 1916, after many years of seeking the Truth and performing numerous ascetic practices, Sotaesan attained great enlightenment. He was twenty-six years old.

Sotaesan's great enlightenment marks the birth of Won Buddhism. The truth of Il-Won—to which Sotaesan had been awakened—became the foundation of the Won Buddhist Order.

Sotaesan chose the image of Il-Won, or One Circle, as the symbol of ultimate reality, which is the origin of the universe and our original nature.

6. BUILDING A LEVEE AT YOUNGSAN

After the enlightenment of Sotaesan many people became his disciples and students.

In April 1918, Sotaesan and nine disciples began to build a levee on a deserted, muddy beach at Youngsan, his hometown. These twenty-two acres of fertile land would soon provide a livelihood for the budding Won Buddhist community.

Through this project, Sotaesan revealed a new model of life and practice: "Practitioners in the future should practice and work together in tandem... Future religious practice must save both the body and the mind."

7. RECEIVING DHARMA APPROVAL

After completing the embankment project, Sotaesan asked his nine disciples to offer prayers for the deliverance of all beings. This fervent prayer began in March 1919, and continued through August of that year.

Their single mind and heart, and their selfless and dedicated spirit, touched the realm of universal truth. Through their prayer, Won Buddhism received approval from the dharma realm. Their spirit of selfless service and sacrifice for the benefit of all beings became the spiritual foundation of Won Buddhism.

8. DRAFTING THE WON BUDDHIST TEACHINGS

From 1920 to 1924, at Bongnae Hermitage in Byonsan, Sotaesan created a new dharma to help liberate all beings from suffering.

Through his vision, traditional buddhadharma was modernized and re-envisioned so that followers of his teaching could attain and use the Great Way without leaving their secular lives. The outline of Sotaesan's new teaching was two-pronged: *The Essential Way of Human Life*, comprised of The Fourfold Grace and Four Essentials, and *The Essential Way of Practice*, comprised of the Threefold Practice and the Eight Articles.

9. SPREADING THE DHARMA AT SHINYONG

In 1924, Sotaesan established a spiritual community at Shinyong, Iksan, to attain the goal of liberating all beings from suffering. This area flourished and later became the headquarters of Won Buddhism, where Sotaesan and his followers worked, practiced, and studied dharma together. Their way of life modeled Sotaesan's teaching: "Buddhadharma is Daily Life, Daily Life is Buddhadharma."

Sotaesan taught that a living religion or practice should not be separate from daily life.

10. ENTERING NIRVANA IN 1943

On June 1, 1943, in Iksan, Sotaesan passed away at the age of fifty-three, having spent twenty-eight years delivering countless dharma to save all sentient beings from suffering.

A year before his passing, Sotaesan finished writing *The Principal Book of Won Buddhism*. The following is his dharma transmission verse:

> *"Being into nonbeing and nonbeing into being,*
> *Turning and turning in the ultimate,*
> *Being and nonbeing are both empty,*
> *Yet this emptiness is also complete."*

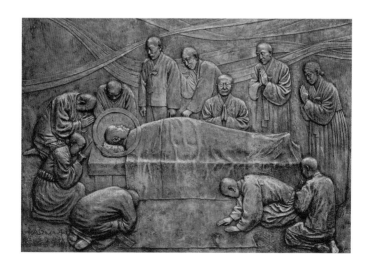

BIBLIOGRAPHY

WORKS IN ENGLISH

Chon, Pal Khn, trans. *The Scripture of Won Buddhism*. Iksan: Won Kwang Publishing Co., 1988.

Yoo, Dosung. *Thunderous Silence*. Boston: Wisdom Publications, 2013.

The Scriptures of Won-Buddhism. Iksan: Won Kwang Publishing Co., 2006.

WORKS IN KOREAN

All excerpts in this book were translated into English by the translators.

The Scripture of Wonbulkyo. Iksan: Won Kwang Publishing Co., 1993.

Daesan. *The Essence of the Won Buddhist Canon*. Iksan: Won Kwang Publishing Co., 1996.

About the Author

Venerable Wolsan

After Venerable Wolsan entered the Won Buddhist faith, he served as the head minister of many Won Buddhist Temples in Korea and also served on the Supreme Council.

He has dedicated his whole life to making Won Buddhist teachings accessible to as many people as possible.

Venerable Wolsan has authored many books, including *Master Chongsan*, *The Stories of Sotaesan*, *The Guide for Mind Training*, *We Harvest What We Sow*, and *My Dream and My Life*.

ABOUT THE TRANSLATORS

Reverend Dosung Yoo

Reverend Dosung Yoo is a teacher and lecturer of meditation, Buddhism, and the Won Buddhist dharma in the United States and in Korea. He currently serves as the Director of the Won Dharma Center in Claverack, New York.

He is a writer, editor, and translator: the author of *Thunderous Silence: A Formula for Ending Suffering* and *The Essence of Won Buddhism*; publisher and translator of *The Method of Sitting Meditation; Tales of a Modern Sage; The Moon Rises in Empty Space;* and *The Principles for Training the Mind.*

Kathy Abeyatunge

Kathy Abeyatunge, dharma name Won JiYeon, joined the Won Dharma Center in Claverack, NY in 2014 and became ordained as a Lay Minister (Wonmu) on January 7, 2024.

She dedicates herself to drawing on the profound yet simple and practical teachings of Won Buddhism to spread the dharma of Timeless and Placeless meditation in daily life.

In 2024, she translated Venerable Wolsan's book into English: *The Essence of Won Buddhism*.